Talking about

Racism

Jen Green

RAINTREE
STECK-VAUGHN
PUBLISHERS
A Steck-Vaughn Company

Austin, Texas
www.steck-vaughn.com

Titles in the series

Talking about …

Adoption • Alcohol • Animal Rights • Bullying Death • Disability • Drugs • Family Breakup Our Environment • Racism

Published by Raintree Steck-Vaughn Publishers,
an imprint of Steck-Vaughn Company

Library of Congress Cataloging-in-Publication Data
Green, Jen.
Racism / Jen Green.
    p.   cm.—(Talking about)
    Includes bibliographical references and index.
    ISBN 0-7398-1375-7
    1. Racism—Juvenile literature.
    [1. Racism.]
    I. Title. II. Series.   305.8
                              G

Printed in Italy. Bound in the United States.
1 2 3 4 5 6 7 8 9 0 03 02 01 00 99

Picture acknowledgments
The publishers acknowledge the following for allowing their photographs to be used: Chapel Studios 4/Oliver Cockell, 19/Graham Horner; Getty Images 5/Mary Kate Denny; Robert Harding 8, 26/R. Cundy; Skjold 14. Photographs on the following pages were taken for the publisher by: Gareth Boden *title page*, 6, 9, 15, 17, 21, 22, 24, 27, 29; Martyn Chillmaid *contents*, 10, 11, 12, 13, 16, 18 (both), 20, 23, 25, 28 (both); Rupert Horrox 7. Cover picture by Angela Hampton.

The publishers would like to thank the children, parents and teachers of St. Stephen's First and Middle School, and the Sandra Reynolds Model Agency. All the people featured in the photographs are models, and are opposed to racism in any form.

Contents

Everyone's Different   4

What Is Racism?   6

Judging Other People   8

How Are People Racist?   10

Why Are People Racist?   12

One of the Gang   14

Is Racism New?   16

How Is Racism
  Passed On?   18

How Does Racism Make
  People Feel?   20

How Can I Deal With
  Racism?   22

How Can We Help Stop
  Racism?   24

Beating Racism
  Together   26

Notes for Parents
  and Teachers   28

Glossary   30

Books to Read   31

Index   32

Everyone's Different

Kate and Leah are best friends. Kate's family is Irish, and Leah's family originally came from Africa. The two girls look different, but they enjoy doing the same things.

Most of us enjoy the differences between people and think they make life more interesting.

But some people treat people from other cultures badly. This is called racism.

What Is Racism?

Racism is saying or doing something to hurt someone who comes from a different culture.

Treating people unfairly just because their skin is a different color from yours is one kind of racism.

Racism isn't just about skin color. It can also be disliking someone because he or she comes from a different country or has a different religion.

Judging Other People

We all have our own likes and dislikes. Josh and James are twins. They look alike, but they enjoy different things. Josh likes reading. James prefers going out on his bike.

When people are racist, they judge other
people by their skin color, culture, or religion,
without finding out what they are really like.

How Are People Racist?

Racism is a kind of bullying. One day, Fatima heard Megan and Sarah laughing about the clothes she wore.

Making fun of the way people dress or talk can be racism.

People can be racist by pushing, fighting, and calling other people bad names.

But racism can also be ignoring someone and never including them in activities.

Why Are People Racist?

When Rosa went to her friend Mai's house for a meal, she had fun learning how to use chopsticks.

Some people feel frightened when they have to try new things or see things they don't understand. Feeling frightened can sometimes make people behave in a racist way.

Some people use racism as a way of blaming others for their problems or disappointments.

Tom blamed Iqbal when he wasn't picked for the soccer team at school.

One of the Gang

Are you in a gang? Being in a gang can be fun. But sometimes people take part in bullying or racism, just to feel as if they are part of a gang.

Peter's gang liked picking on Lee. Michael was worried that, if he tried to stop them, they might pick on him instead.

Is Racism New?

Racism is not new. Hundreds of years ago, people from Europe sailed across the oceans. They took control of the lands they found. They treated the people who already lived there badly.

In Africa, for example, Europeans made many Africans become slaves and were cruel to them.

Later, people all over the world worked to end slavery because they realized it was wrong.

How Is Racism Passed On?

One day Sophie's older sister Amy
made a joke about black people.

Later, Sophie repeated
to her best friend
what Amy had said.

No one is born with racist ideas. We pick up ideas from our families and friends or from newspapers, radio, and TV.

How Does Racism Make People Feel?

Racism is very hurtful and upsetting. When Megan and Sarah laughed at her, Fatima felt angry. Fatima had thought they were all friends.

When Peter bullied Lee, Lee felt scared. He spent time at night worrying about the gang.

How Can I Deal With Racism?

It's not easy to deal with racism. You may feel very angry, but fighting back often makes things worse. Teresa and Maria decided to walk away from Peter's gang.

Fatima decided to stand up for herself.
She told the bullies to leave her alone.
First, she practiced in front of a mirror.

How Can We Help Stop Racism?

It can be hard to keep people from being racist. But if you say nothing, it will look as if you agree with them.

Michael stood up for Lee. Together, they told Peter that if the bullying didn't stop, they would tell a teacher.

Sometimes the best thing to do is tell a grownup. If the first person you tell doesn't help, try someone else.

Beating Racism Together

We are all part of one race—the human race. But racism divides people. Don't judge people before you know them. Find out what they are really like instead.

Say no to racism whenever you can.
Everyone has a right to your respect.
No one should have to feel afraid.

Notes for Parents and Teachers

As you read this book with a child or with a group of children, you may find it useful to stop and discuss the issues that come up in the text.

Ask the children whether they personally have ever experienced racism. Have they ever felt that someone else was being racist? Stress that racism can take many different forms, from name-calling and ignoring someone to physical bullying. If they have experienced or witnessed racism, how did they feel and react? Emphasize the importance of talking about feelings, with friends or a trusted adult.

Using role play, children can explore different ways of dealing with racism. Encourage them to act out standing up for themselves, diffusing a situation by walking away, and getting help from others. Emphasize that in many situations, it is best to tell an adult.

Ask the children whether they have ever felt like being racist, or stood by when someone else was behaving in a racist way. Encourage children to think about the effects of their actions on others. Stress that racism is always wrong and must stop. Everyone has a right to be proud of their culture and to feel safe.

If your child has experienced racism at school, listen carefully to what he or she has to say. Then discuss the matter with the principal and find out how the school tackles racism. Advice and support are also available from several organizations. You can also help by reflecting on your own views about racism and realizing that your attitudes can have a great effect on your children.

Glossary

Bullying Doing or saying something to hurt or frighten someone.

Chopsticks Two thin sticks that are used to pick up food. They are often used by people from Asia.

Culture A group of people who share certain ideas and ways of doing things. For example, people from one culture may share the same religious beliefs.

Human race All the people in the world.

Respect Treating others well and showing that you think their feelings are important.

Slaves People who are owned by someone else and forced to work for their owner without being paid.

Twins Two children with the same mother, who are born almost at the same time. Some twins look exactly the same, too.

Books to Read

Birdseye, Debbie Holsclaw. *Under Our Skin: Kids Talk About Race*. New York: Holiday House, 1997.

Gillam, Scott. *Discrimination: Prejudice in Action* (Multicultural Issues). Springfield, NJ: Enslow, 1995.

Green, Jen. *Dealing with Racism* (How Do I Feel About). Ridgefield, CT: Copper Beech Books, 1998.

Hamanaka, Sheila. *The Journey: Japanese Americans, Racism and Renewal*. New York: Orchard Paperbacks, 1995.

Sanders, Pete. *Racism* (What Do You Know About). Ridgefield, CT: Copper Beech, 1995.

Index

Numbers in **bold** refer to pictures as well as text.

Africa 4, 17

blaming others 13
bullying **10**, **11**, **13**, 14, **15**, 21, 23, 24

clothes 10
cultures 5, 6

dealing with racism **22**, **23**

Europeans 16, 17

feelings 12, **20**, **21**, 22, 27
fighting 11, 22

gangs **14**, **15**, 21
getting help **24**, **25**

Ireland 4

jokes 18

name-calling 11

newspapers 19

radio 19
religion 7, 9

skin color 6, 7, 9
slaves 17

TV 19